Eli Thayer

The New England emigrant aid company

and its influence, through the Kansas contest, upon national history

Eli Thayer

The New England emigrant aid company
and its influence, through the Kansas contest, upon national history

ISBN/EAN: 9783744745086

Printed in Europe, USA, Canada, Australia, Japan

Cover: Foto ©ninafisch / pixelio.de

More available books at **www.hansebooks.com**

THE

New England

EMIGRANT AID COMPANY

AND ITS INFLUENCE, THROUGH THE KANSAS CONTEST,

UPON NATIONAL HISTORY.

By ELI THAYER.

WORCESTER, MASS.:

FRANKLIN P. RICE, *Publisher.*

MDCCCLXXXVII

The following pages comprise an abstract of two lectures given before The Worcester Society of Antiquity in March, 1886. Some notes have been added.

THE NEW ENGLAND EMIGRANT AID COMPANY,

AND ITS INFLUENCE, THROUGH THE KANSAS CONTEST,
UPON NATIONAL HISTORY.

History gives abundant proof, that a brief period of time has often determined the character and destiny of a nation. Such a period is properly called its controlling or dominating epoch.

In the history of our own country, the year 1854 holds this commanding position, and governs all our subsequent years. It was in this year that the Slave Power attained its highest eminence, and demolished the last barrier that stood in the way of its complete supremacy and its perpetual dominion. The executive, the legislative and the judicial departments of the Government, were entirely within its power. Not content, however, with the repeal of the Missouri Compromise, which opened all our vast territorial possessions to Slavery; not content with its well assured and absolute power, within our national boundaries, it aspired to annex other countries, and under its direful rule, to build up a vast empire "on the corner-stone of Slavery."

In the same year, 1854, a power, before unknown in the world's history, was created and brought into use, to save to Freedom all our territories, then open by law to the possession and dominion of Slavery. This new power was an ORGANIZED, SELF-SACRIFICING EMIGRATION. Its mission was to dispute with Slavery every square foot of land exposed to its control. A hand-to-hand conflict was to decide between the system of free labor and the system of slave labor.

The repeal of the Missouri Compromise, in May, 1854, proved that the legislative restriction of Slavery was simply a delusion, and that the contest between Freedom and Slavery, if such a contest were yet possible, must be carried on outside of legislative halls. It must be a contest on the prairies, and the power victorious there, would, in due time, govern the country.

Was it possible to bring these two kinds of civilization to a decisive struggle ? Was it possible to arouse the North to effective resistance, after more than thirty years of continuous defeat by the South ?

During all this period of the successful aggression and increasing strength of Slavery, there was in the North corresponding apprehension and alarm. On the repeal of the Missouri Compromise this apprehension became despondency, and this alarm became despair.

There were in the Northern States two agencies professedly hostile to Slavery. One was political, and opposed Slavery extension in a legal way, by means of legislative restriction. The other was sentimental and contended for the overthrow of Slavery by revolutionary methods — advocating the dissolution of the Union as the best and only sure way to this result. The first of these two agencies was the Free Soil party, which was first formed in 1848, and put into shape for political action by the convention that nominated Martin Van Buren and Charles Francis Adams. This new party drew its supporters, in about equal numbers, from the Whig and Democratic parties, while it completely absorbed a feeble political organization, which at the time had a kind of nebulous existence under the name of the Liberty party.

From the time of its creation, in 1848, to the day of the repeal of the Missouri Compromise, in 1854, the Free Soil party had scarcely increased at all, either in influence or numbers. Its purpose was to insert in every act of Congress opening a territory to settlement, a provision to forever exclude Slavery therefrom.* This seemed to its supporters to be a legal, practical way of stopping the extension of Slavery, by preventing the

* The Wilmot Proviso.

making of more slave states. This new party had no sympathy whatever with disunionists, and proposed to act against Slavery in accordance with the Laws, the Constitution and the Union.

But the Slave Power had acquired such ascendency in the Government, that the new party never once applied its slavery-excluding method. On the contrary, after six years of political life, which were six years of active effort and earnest appeals for free labor in our territories, it was obliged to witness the complete overthrow and utter ruin of its cardinal principle, in the repeal of the Missouri Compromise. This action of Congress at once convinced the new party, not only of the futility of its methods, but also of its own feebleness and utter inability to cope successfully with Slavery.

Its leaders were silent in their despair, or spoke only to lament their defeat and the rapidly approaching calamities of the nation. They had no plan to propose for future action.

> " There was silence deep as death,
> While we floated on our path ;
> And the boldest held his breath
> For a time. "

Of the matter involved in the repeal of the Missouri Compromise and the passage of the Kansas-Nebraska bill, Mr. Sumner had said in the United States Senate, 24th of February, 1854 :

"The question presented for your consideration is not surpassed in grandeur by any that has occurred in our national history since the Declaration of Independence. In every aspect it assumes gigantic proportions, whether we simply consider the extent of territory it concerns, or the public faith and national policy which it assails, or that higher question — that *Question of Questions*, as far above others as Liberty is above the common things of life —which it opens anew for judgment."

The following views of their ablest champions prove how hopeless and humiliated they had become.

Said William H. Seward, in the United States Senate, May 25th, 1854, the day of the repeal of the Missouri Compromise :

"The sun has set for the last time upon the guaranteed and certain liberties of all the unsettled and unorganized portions of the American Continent that lie within the jurisdiction of the United States. To-morrow's sun will rise in dim eclipse over them. How long that obscuration shall last, is known only to the Power that directs and controls all human events. For myself, I know only this, that no human power can prevent its coming on, and that its passing off will be hastened and secured by others than those now here, and perhaps by only those belonging to future generations.

" Sir, it would be almost factious to offer further resistance to this measure here. Indeed successful resistance was never expected to be made in this Hall. The Senate is an old battle ground, on which have been fought many contests, and always, at least since 1820, with fortune adverse to the cause of equal and universal freedom. "

Mr. Wade said :

"The humiliation of the North is complete and overwhelming. No Southern enemy of hers can wish her deeper degradation. "

Mr. Chase said :

" This bill, doubtless paves the way for the approach of new, alarming and perhaps fatal dangers to our country. "

From the New York *Tribune*, 14th March, 1854 :

" We as a nation are ruled by the Black Power. It is composed of tyrants. See then how the North is always beaten. The Black Power is a unit. It is a steady, never-failing force. It is a real power. Thus far it has been the only unvarying power of the country, for it never surrenders and never wavers. It has always governed and now governs more than ever."

The New York *Tribune*, in an editorial, on the 24th of June, well expressed the feeling of despondency at the North :

" Not even by accident, is any advantage left for liberty in their bill. It is all blackness without a single gleam of light, a desert without one spot of verdure, a crime that can show no redeeming point. "

So much then for the political anti-slavery agency.

The other agency against Slavery was the sentimental one established and led by William Lloyd Garrison. It was much older than the one already considered, but inferior in numbers and far more inferior in influence. Its champions advocated Disunion as the " corner-stone of all true anti-slavery." They shall speak for themselves.

Wendell Phillips at the A. A. S. Convention in the Tabernacle, New York City, May 4th, 1848, offered the following resolution which was passed :

" That this Society deems it a duty to reiterate its convictions that the only exodus of the slave out of his present house of bondage is OVER THE RUINS OF THE PRESENT AMERICAN CHURCH, AND THE PRESENT AMERICAN UNION."

In May, 1856, Mr. Garrison offered the following resolution at a meeting of the Massachusetts Anti-Slavery Society :

" *Resolved :* That the one great issue before the country is, THE DISSOLUTION OF THE UNION, in comparison with which all other issues with the Slave Power are as dust in the balance ; therefore we will give ourselves to the work of annulling this ' covenant with death ' as essential to our own innocency, and the speedy and everlasting overthrow of the Slave System."

The following was also adopted by the Abolitionists in New York City in December, 1859 :

"*Resolved :* That we invite a free correspondence with the Disunionists of the South, in order to devise the most suitable way and means to secure the dissolution of the present imperfect and inglorious union between the free and slave States." *

* But when Secession had become, in the minds of the enemies of the nation, an accomplished deed, Mr. Garrison and his associates, in the face of the aroused people of the North, had sense enough not to insult the outraged sentiment of their section by further avowal of their sympathy with Disunion. They respected the halter too much. Soon we see them on the other tack ; and when the war was over they were the loudest in the jubilee over the restoration of the "grand and glorious Union" which they, and they alone, had saved! After the war Mr. Garrison said : "I am with the President [Johnson], and desire to make treason infamous."—See *Century* Magazine for February, 1887, Vol. xxxiii., page 638, note.

With such views and purposes the people of the Northern
States had no sympathy. The Abolitionists, no doubt, had
good motives, but their judgment was invariably bad. Their
methods were everywhere condemned. They never attained to
the dignity or influence of a party or even a faction. They
were a cabal, active, noisy and pugnacious, but never effective.
By their own showing a quarter of a century spent in denouncing the church, the clergy and the Union had accomplished nothing. Slavery had grown stronger every day, while opposition
to it had not increased at all. Massachusetts was as sound an
anti-slavery state before they were born as it has ever been
since. But she was for legal and constitutional methods only,
and always for the Union.

In 1787, Nathan Dane, one of our representatives in Congress,
revived the ordinance, introduced three years earlier by Thomas
Jefferson, and secured its passage. This was to make the great
North-West free territory forever. All this was before Garrison was born! But such anti-slavery action was not repeated
during the entire period of Mr. Garrison's efforts for disunion.
In all that time, Slavery was unrestricted, and made steady progress. But some say he was "the father of anti-slavery"
in the United States. Some say Lundy was. So there
is a dispute. Mr. A says, Ponce de Leon discovered America.
Mr. B says no; it was Pizarro. While A and B get red in the
face, the rest of the alphabet can afford to remain unmoved.

Slavery never had a legal existence in Massachusetts.
The people never wanted it and always hated it. They
hated its adjuncts and attendants of manacles, blood-hounds
and auction blocks, as much before Garrison was born, as they
did after he had pictured them, in the *Liberator*, for twenty-five
years. This incessant pecking at the leaves and twigs of the
upas tree of Slavery, seemed to them to stimulate rather
than retard its growth. The Northern people ardently desired
to destroy the tree itself, and were ready to adopt any legal and
constitutional plan which might do this work. Garrison's
method of casting out a devil by splitting the patient in
two lengthwise, they did not approve — for two reasons :

1st, Because the patient would die ;
2nd, Because the devil would live.

Still the Abolitionists boasted constantly of increasing numbers. Every new subscriber to the *Liberator*, every new face in their annual or quarterly conventions, was proof to them of the rapid increase of disunionists; as if every one who reads the flaming poster of the coming circus is an acrobat! as if every one who witnesses the exhibition is an actor within the ring!

Some friends of the Abolitionists still claim that Garrison and his associates founded the Liberty and Free Soil parties. This claim is the exact opposite of the truth. They opposed both of these parties, and hated their champions more than they hated the slaveholders themselves. They constantly abused every leading anti-slavery man who was not a disunionist. Ample proof of this can be seen in the editorials of the *Liberator* against Horace Mann, Salmon P. Chase and Dr. Bellows. Lincoln, Seward, Wade, Sumner and Wilson were not spared. * About the time of Sumner's death, Mr. Garrison went before a committee of the Massachusetts Legislature to protest against expunging some foolish resolutions on record denouncing that famous senator, he claiming that Mr. Sumner had not amounted to much in the anti-slavery struggle! †

But why prolong the description? Let the Abolitionists draw their own portraits. They still exist in the columns of the *Liberator*, the birth-place and the sepulchre of all their plans and

* At a meeting of the Worcester County South Division A. S. Society held at Worcester, Aug. 12, 1860, Parker Pillsbury offered the following resolution, which was adopted:

" *Resolved:* That in the two recently published speeches of Charles Sumner, we see the blinding, bewildering and depraving effect of American politics, and of contact with slave-holders—the former, made in the U. S. Senate, being a four hours' argument against the 'five-headed barbarism of slavery,' and repudiated by many of the leaders of Republicanism; and the latter a full admission of the constitutionality of slave-holding, and an eloquent argument in favor of the election of Lincoln and Hamlin, both of whom believe in slave-hunting as well as slave-holding, and who virtually declare in their platform that the noble John Brown was one of the gravest criminals who ever died by a halter."

† See *Warrington Pen Portraits*, page 366.

purposes. That paper is also an arsenal, amply sufficient to furnish arms to a million of their assailants. It gives abundant proof of the following statements :

With all their keenness of vision, the Abolitionists never saw anything as it was. With all their eloquence they never advocated any cause to a successful issue. With all their prophetic power and practice they never predicted any event which came to pass. With all their love of freedom, they constantly increased the burdens of the slaves. Demanding immediate emancipation, they strove to retard the overthrow of slavery. Contending for the dissolution of the Union as the only means of destroying Slavery, they saw Slavery destroyed not only without their aid, but against their protest, while the Union was preserved and made permanent and harmonious.* Incessantly denouncing

---

* The following letter, written by Col. Asa H. Waters a short time before his death, is so conclusive in its statements, that it may appropriately be given a place here.

" MILLBURY, Nov. 20th, 1886.

" MR. THAYER,

" Dear Sir:— When the Free Soil Party was formed in '48 Garrison and his party had labored seventeen years and failed to carry a single town in New England. In one year we put ninety members into the Legislature, the second year we carried Worcester County, and the third year put a *Jupiter Tonans*—Charles Sumner—into the very citadel of the slave power. Then, at a convention in Worcester, Wilson had the party christened the Republican Party with the same Free Soil platform, and on that we elected Lincoln President, and he abolished Slavery.

" In all this, we had the bitter opposition of Garrison and his party, which finally clasped hands with the Disunionists of the South, in a determined effort to break up the Union. Had they succeeded, so far from abolishing slavery, they would have vastly extended it. The design of the South was to cope in New Mexico, Arizona, Indian Territory, Utah and Southern California, and thus build up a great Southern Empire founded on Slavery. I enclose the resolution, in which they proposed the unholy alliance. A committee was chosen, and I think M. D Conway was chairman. The correspondence was never published. Secession movements soon after commenced, and in a little over a year the war broke out. It was suppressed and slavery abolished by the patriotic *Union Sentiment of the North*, which always was its predominant political sentiment. 'Down with the Disunionists;' 'Death to traitors, slavery or no slavery,' were the cries that rang through the ranks; and for a long time the army returned fugitive slaves. At length it was discovered that the rebels were using their slaves as a means of strength, which made them contraband of war and liable to confiscation. Then their obstinate resistance created a 'military necessity,' and on these two principles rather than by any authority in the United States Constitution, President Lincoln issued his proclamation.

the clergy and churches of the Northern States as the upholders
of Slavery, they lived to see them among the foremost leaders in
its destruction by the methods of the Emigrant Aid Company,
which the Abolitionists hated, ridiculed and opposed.
No other fraternity of mountebanks ever lived so long, or
worked so hard, or did so little.

During the winter of 1854 I was, for the second time, a Representative from Worcester in the Legislature of Massachusetts.
I had felt to some degree the general alarm in anticipa-
tion of the repeal of the Missouri Compromise, but not
the depression and despondency that so affected others who regarded the cause of liberty as hopelessly lost. As the
winter wore away, I began to have a conviction which came to
be ever present, that something *must* be done to end the domi-
nation of Slavery. I felt a personal responsibility, and though
I long struggled to evade the question, I found it to be impossi-
ble. I pondered upon it by day, and dreamed of it by
night. By what plan could this great problem be solved ?
What force could be effectively opposed to the power that seemed about to spread itself over the continent ? Suddenly,
it came upon me like a revelation. It was ORGANIZED AND
ASSISTED EMIGRATION.* Then came the question, was it possi-

The abolitionists opposed his election, and being non-resistants, were rarely
found in the ranks, and they thus failed for the most part to become identified with
the active forces that abolished slavery.
"And yet, for twenty years the press has been teeming with their effusions in
poetry and prose, to convince the world that they abolished slavery! They have
done much to falsify history, and produce wrong impressions on the rising generation. A duty devolves on those who know the facts, to counteract and set back this
tide. But how shall it be done? Where is the press that can be enlisted?
"I had a long controversy with Oliver Johnson; he finally jumped the fence and
cleared from the field, declaring he never made the issue that Garrison abolished
slavery. The editor (Slack) said he did. He boasted of being 'a member of the
Republican Party.' In the Greeley campaign of '72 against Grant, he labored with
his Southern allies and they carried six Southern states, but no Northern. That
shows his consistency. "Yours Respectfully,
"A. H. WATERS."
* The Kansas emigration was emphatically a self-*sacrificing* emigration — a power hitherto unknown in history. All previous emigrations had been either forced or
voluntary, and if voluntary were self-*seeking*.

ble to create such an agency to save Kansas ? I believed the time for such a noble and heroic development had come ; but could hope be inspired, and the pulsations of life be started beneath the ribs of death? The projected plan would call upon men to risk life and property in establishing freedom in Kansas. They would be called to pass over millions of acres of better land than any in the disputed territory was supposed to be, and where peace and plenty were assured, to meet the revolver and the bowie knife defending Slavery and assailing Freedom. Could such men be found, they would certainly prove themselves to be the very highest type of Christian manhood, as much above all other emigrants, as angels are above men. *Could* such men be found?

It happened, that on the evening of the 11th of March, 1854, there was a large meeting in the City Hall in Worcester, to protest against the passage of the Kansas-Nebraska Bill, and the repeal of the Missouri Compromise. I attended the meeting, and not having yet taken counsel of anyone, determined to see how the plan would be received by an intelligent New England audience without any preparation for the announcement. Accordingly, making the last speech of the evening I for the first time disclosed the plan. The Worcester *Spy* of March 13th, has the conclusion of my speech as follows :

"It is time now to think of what is to be done in the event of the passage of the Kansas-Nebraska Bill. Now is the time to organize an opposition, that will utterly defeat the schemes of the selfish men who misrepresent the nation at Washington. Let every effort be made and every appliance be brought to bear, to fill up that vast and fertile territory, with free men — with men who hate slavery, and who will drive the hideous thing from the broad and beautiful plains where they go to raise their free homes. [Loud cheers.]

"I for one am willing to be taxed one fourth of my time or of my earnings, until this be done — until a barrier of free hearts and strong hands shall be built around the land our fathers consecrated to freedom, to be her heritage forever. [Loud cheers.]"

If instead of this impetuous, spontaneous and enthusiastic response there had been only a moderate approbation of the plan, you would never have heard of the Emigrant Aid Company. The citizens of Worcester were sponsors at its baptism, and upon their judgment I implicitly relied, and I was not deceived. I did not expect that all who applauded would go to Kansas, or even that any of them would go, but I knew that whatever a Worcester audience would applaud in that manner I could find men to perform. There was no more doubt in my mind from that time.

Without further delay I drew up the charter of the "Massachusetts Emigrant Aid Company," and by personal solicitation secured the corporators. I introduced the matter in the Legislature and had it referred to the committee on the judiciary, of which James D. Colt, afterwards a justice of the State Supreme Court, was chairman. At the hearing I appeared before the committee and said in behalf of the petition :

" This is a plan to prevent the forming of any more slave states. If you will give us the charter there shall never be another slave state admitted into the Union. In the halls of Congress we have been invariably beaten for more than thirty years, and it is now time to change the battle-ground from Congress to the prairies, where we shall invariably triumph."

Mr. Colt replied :

" We are willing to gratify you, by reporting favorably your charter; but we all believe it to be impracticable and utterly futile. Here you are fifteen hundred miles from the battle ground, while the most thickly settled portion of Missouri lies on the eastern border of Kansas, and can in one day blot out all you can do in a year. Neither can you get men who now have peaceful and happy homes in the East to risk the loss of everything by going to Kansas. "

But Mr. Colt reported in favor of the charter, and it passed, though it cost its author much labor, for not one member either of the Senate or House had any faith in the measure.

The following is the first section of the charter :

" SEC. 1. Benjamin C. Clark, Isaac Livermore, Charles Allen, Isaac Davis, William G. Bates, Stephen C. Phillips, Charles C. Hazewell, Alexander H. Bullock, Henry Wilson, James S. Whitney,

Samuel E. Sewall, Samuel G. Howe, James Holland, Moses Kimball, James D. Green, Francis W. Bird, Otis Clapp, Anson Burlingame, Eli Thayer and Otis Rich, their associates, successors and assigns, are hereby made a corporation, by the name of the Massachusetts Emigrant Aid Company, for the purpose of assisting emigrants to settle in the West ; and for this purpose, they have all the powers and privileges, and be subject to all the duties, restrictions and liabilities, set forth in the thirty-eighth and forty-fourth chapters of the Revised Statutes.

The charter was signed by the Governor on the 26th day of April. On the 4th of May a meeting was held at the State House, by the corporators and others, and a committee chosen to report a plan of organization and work. This committee consisted of Eli Thayer, Alexander H. Bullock and Edward E. Hale of Worcester, Richard Hildreth and Otis Clapp of Boston. They made a report at an adjourned meeting showing the proposed operation of the enterprise, of which the following is an extract :

" The Emigrant Aid Company has been incorporated to protect emigrants, as far as may be, from the inconveniences we have enumerated. Its duty is to organize emigration to the West and bring it into a system. This duty, which should have been attempted long ago, is particularly essential now in the critical position of the Western Territories.

" The Legislature has granted a charter, with a capital sufficient for these purposes. This capital is not to exceed $5,000,000. In no single year are assessments to a larger amount than ten per cent. to be called for. The corporators believe that if the company be organized at once, as soon as the subscriptions to the stock amounts to $1,000,000, the annual income to be derived from that amount, and the subsequent subscriptions, may be so appropriated as to render most essential service to the emigrants ; to plant a free state in Kansas, to the lasting advantage of the country ; and to return a handsome profit to the stockholders upon their investment.

.   .   .   .

" To accomplish the object in view, it is recommended, 1st, that the Directors contract immediately with some one of the competing lines of travel for the conveyance of twenty thousand persons from the northern and middle states, to that place in the West which the Directors shall select for their first settlement.

" It Is believed that passage may be obtained, in so large a contract, at half the price paid by individuals. We recommend that emigrants receive the full advantage of this diminution in price, and that they be forwarded in companies of two hundred, as they apply, at these reduced rates of travel.

" 2d. It is recommended that at such points as the Directors select for places of settlement, they shall at once construct a boarding-house or receiving-house, in which three hundred persons may receive temporary accommodation on their arrival—and that the number of such houses be enlarged as necessity may dictate. The new comers or their families may thus be provided for in the necessary interval which elapses while they are making their selection of a location.

" 3d. It is recommended that the Directors procure and send forward steam saw-mills, and such other machines as shall be of constant service in a new settlement, which cannot, however, be purchased or carried out conveniently by individual settlers. These machines may be leased or run by the company's agents. At the same time it is desirable that a printing press be sent out, and a weekly newspaper established. This would be the organ of the company's agents ; would extend information regarding its settlement; and be from the very first an index of that love of freedom and of good morals which it is to be hoped may characterize the State now to be formed.

" 4th. It is recommended that the company's agents locate and take up for the company's benefit the sections of land in which the boarding-houses and mills are located, and no others. And further, that whenever the Territory shall be organized as a Free State, the Directors shall dispose of all its interests, then replace, by the sales, the money laid out, declare a dividend to the stockholders, and

" 5th. That they then select a new field, and make similar arrangements for the settlement and organization of another Free State of this Union.

.   .   .   .

" Under the plan proposed, it will be but two or three years before the Company can dispose of its property in the territory first occupied — and reimburse itself for its first expenses. At that time, in a State of 70,000 inhabitants, it will possess several reservations of 640 acres each, on which are boarding houses and mills, and the churches and schools which it has rendered necessary. From these centers will the settlements of the State have radiated. In other words, these points will then be the large commercial positions of the new State. If there were only one such, its value, after the region should be so far peopled, would make a very large dividend to the company which sold it, besides restoring the original capital with which to enable it to attempt the same adventure elsewhere.

. . . .

"It is recommended that a meeting of the stockholders be called on the first Wednesday in June, to organize the company for one year, and that the corporators at this time, make a temporary organization, with power to obtain subscriptions to the stock and make any necessary preliminary arrangements.

"ELI THAYER,
For the Committee."

It will be seen by the above that the enterprise was intended to be a money-making affair as well as a philanthropic undertaking. The fact that we intended to make it pay the investors pecuniarily brought upon us the reproaches and condemnation of some of the Abolitionists, at least one of whom declared in my hearing that he had rather give over the territory to Slavery than to make a cent out of the operation of saving it to Freedom. In all my emigration schemes I intended to make the results return a profitable dividend in cash.

In pursuance of the last recommendation of the above report, the corporators made a temporary organization by the choice of Eli Thayer as President *pro tem.*, and Dr. Thomas H. Webb, of Boston, as Secretary; and opened books of subscription in Boston, Worcester and New York.

The capital stock of the Massachusetts Company was originally fixed at $5,000,000, from which it was proposed to collect an assessment of four per cent. for the operations of 1854, as soon as $1,000,000 had been subscribed. Books for stock subscriptions were opened and the undertaking was fairly started. I felt confident that even a few colonies from the North would make the freedom of Kansas a necessity; for the whole power of the free states would be ready to protect their sons in that territory.

I at once hired Chapman Hall in Boston, and began to speak day and evening in favor of the enterprise. I also addressed meetings elsewhere, and labored in every possible way to make converts to my theory.

Not only was a new plan proposed but it was advocated by new arguments, some points of which were as follows:

The present crisis was to decide whether Freedom or Slavery should rule our country for centuries to come. That Slavery was a great national curse; that it practically ruined one half of the nation and greatly impeded the progress of the other half. That it was a curse to the negro, but a much greater curse to white men. It made the slaveholders petty tyrants who had no correct idea of themselves or of anybody else. It made the poor whites of the South more abject and degraded than the slaves themselves. That it was an insurmountable obstacle in the way of the nation's progress and prosperity. That it must be overcome and extirpated. That the way to do this was to go to the prairies of Kansas and show the superiority of free labor civilization; to go with all our free labor trophies: churches and schools, printing presses, steam engines and mills; and in a peaceful contest convince every poor man from the South of the superiority of free labor. That it was much better to *go* and *do* something for free labor than to stay at home and talk of manacles and auction-blocks and blood-hounds, while deploring the never-ending aggressions of slavery. That in this contest the South had not one element of success. We had much greater numbers, much greater wealth, greater readiness of organization and better facilities of migration. That we should put a cordon of Free States from Minnesota to the Gulf of Mexico, and stop the forming of Slave States. After that we should colonize the northern border Slave States and exterminate Slavery. That our work was not to make women and children cry in anti-slavery conventions, by sentimental appeals, BUT TO GO AND PUT AN END TO SLAVERY.* '

* The Garrisonians opposed everybody and everything outside of their little clique, and were led into many ridiculous inconsistencies. A specimen disunion resolution is here given:

"*Resolved:* That in our judgment, the dissolution of the present Union with the slaveholding states, presents the only peaceable remedy for the evils of slavery, and the surest pledge of its entire abolition; inasmuch as, then, the slaveholders, unable alone to hold their slaves, must devise immediate measures for emancipation," etc.

At the close of one of the meetings in Boston, a man in the rear of the hall arose and announced his intention of subscribing $10,000 towards the capital stock of the company. This was John M. S. Williams of Cambridgeport, who was afterwards prominently connected with the Emigrant Aid Company. Charles Francis Adams came forward with a subscription of $25,000, and others followed. It was at one of the Chapman Hall meetings that I first saw Charles Robinson, (afterwards Governor of Kansas,) and engaged him to act as agent of the Emigrant Aid Company, in Kansas. A wiser and more sagacious man for this work could not have been found within the borders of the nation.

Towards the end of May, leaving the subscription books with the secretary of the company, I went to New York, to secure the aid and coöperation of prominent gentlemen of that city. I called upon Horace Greeley and set forth the plan in all its details. The matter was entirely new to him, and made a most favorable impression on his judgment. He unhesitatingly gave it his heartiest support, and entered into the scheme with great enthusiasm. The New York *Tribune* of May 29th, 1854, contained a lengthy account of the organization and purpose of the Massachusetts Emigrant Aid Company, with the charter and report of the commit-

When, however, the Emigrant Aid Company announced its purpose to form a cordon of free States around the slave territory, and thus prevent by actual occupation, at least the spread of Slavery, the Garrisonians turned squarely around and faced the other way, as witness the following "Resolution:"

"*Resolved:* That the idea of starving slavery to death by confining it within its present limits, is, in view of the fact, that the larger part of the territory already secured to the Slave Power, is, as yet, virgin soil, on which it can grow and fatten for ages to come; a most dangerous delusion."

Prof. Spring, in his history of Kansas, ludicrously speaks of the Garrisonians as "solitary knights bestriding —

'The winged Hippogriff, Reform.' "

He errs, however, in saying that the integration of the Northern Anti-Slavery sentiment was due to them. They never did anything but disintegrate it, by changing a few weak-minded Anti-Slavery men into rabid Disuntonists. The integration of the Northern sentiment was brought about by the Kansas contest and the means that sustained it.

tee, printed in full. The following is an extract from his editorial :

" Such, in brief, is the plan offered to the earnest and philanthropic men of the free states who desire to prevent the spread of slavery into Kansas and Nebraska, and to secure the early admission of those territories into the Union as Free States. To all those who are anxious to do something in the present crisis to repair the wrong just committed at Washington, it offers a wide and hopeful field of effort. Here is abundant opportunity for all who have money to invest or a heart to labor in the great cause of Freedom. The scheme strikes us as singularly well adapted to secure the objects in view. Properly managed and in the hands of discreet and responsible men, it cannot fail to accomplish the noble and generous purpose at which it aims, and at the same time it promises to eventually return to every contributor, all of his original outlay, with a handsome recompense for its use. From this plan, thus briefly shadowed forth, we entertain a confident hope of the most satisfactory results, and cordially commend it to public attention. "

This was followed by a series of powerful editorials, which fully unfolded the new " Plan of Freedom, " as Mr. Greeley called it, and set forth its merits in a forcible and convincing manner, urging the formation of Emigrant Societies throughout the North.

In the *Tribune* of May 30th, he says :

" THE PLAN OF FREEDOM set forth in yesterday's *Tribune* has been eagerly seized upon by some of our best and most distinguished citizens, and a private preliminary meeting will be immediately held in furtherance of its suggestions. . . . . . .

" The organization of a powerful association of large capital, in the aid of human freedom, is a step in a new direction of philanthropic effort which may well enlist the sympathies of the unselfish and benevolent, not only of this country, but of all mankind.

" In view of the monstrous wrongs that slavery is at this hour meditating, in view of the enormity it has just perpetrated, the heart of every man who has one spark of humanity in his bosom, must be stirred, as with the sound of a trumpet, by the suggestion of a remedy so simple, so comprehensive and so practical. . . .

" The great labors of the world have been performed by association. Our societies for the spread of the Bible, and the diffusion of Christianity — and our other varied combinations for benevolent objects — all demonstrate the immense power of well-directed associative effort."

In New York I had no difficulty in enlisting supporters of the scheme among the most prominent and influential citizens, as the following names will show. These gentlemen attended my meetings, and aided liberally in a pecuniary way to further the cause :

Cyrus Curtis, Moses H. Grinnell, George W. Blunt, John A. King (President of Columbia College), E. D. Morgan, David Dudley Field, Simeon Draper, Isaac Dayton, Benjamin W. Bonney, Le Grand Lockwood, John Bigelow, William C. Noyes, R. W. Blatchford, Lucius Robinson, H. A. Chittenden. These gentlemen were the heartiest endorsers of the enterprise. They were of all shades of political opinion.

At a meeting held in the parlors of George W. Blunt, after I had explained the methods and purposes of the Emigrant Aid Company ; how, if properly supported, it would secure freedom to Kansas and to all the territories, and that Slavery thus circumscribed would lose its political power and be doomed to speedy extinction, a tall and gaunt young man among my hearers arose and said : " I have been called a ' Hunker Whig,' but I am no friend to the extension of slavery. I have waited for a chance to act against it in a legal and constitutional way. Now for the first time in my life I have listened to a practical elucidation of the slavery question involving no questionable methods. So, ' Hunker Whig' though I am called, and poor man though I am — for I am not worth more than four thousand dollars — I will now give Mr. Thayer my check for the Emigrant Aid Company for one thousand dollars." I inquired the name of the gentleman, and some one replied: " WILLIAM M. EVARTS." In 1877 Mr. Evarts sent a message to me, saying: "Tell Mr. Thayer that that thousand dollar subscription was the best investment I ever made in my life."

Editorial from the New York *Tribune* of May 31, 1854 :

" THE PLAN OF FREEDOM which we put forth in Monday's paper already awakens an echo in the public mind. In addition to further active steps of the gentlemen in the city who have taken hold of the subject, we have received voluntary offers of subscription by letter, together with the most fervent expressions of zeal and determination from all quarters to rally in defense of freedom and in opposition to the gigantic schemes of aggression started by the slave power. The contest already takes the form of the People against Tyranny and Slavery. The whole crowd of slave drivers and traitors, backed by a party organization, a corrupt majority in Congress, a soulless partizan press, an administration with its paid officers armed with revolvers, and sustained by the bayonets of a mercenary soldiery, will all together prove totally insufficient to cope with an aroused People.

" We extract from our correspondence as follows :

" ' To the Editor of The New York Tribune :

" ' Having watched with much interest the incipient movements in Massachusetts to form the Emigrant Aid Society, and having great faith in such an enterprise, if confided to proper hands, I am much gratified to find by your paper of this day, that the organization is so far completed as to admit the opening of subscriptions. Wishing to aid the enterprise out of my feeble ability, I request you to insert my name in the subscription for five hundred dollars ($500.) . . . . .

" ' The day of deliverance dawns. The spirit of freedom shall awake.

" ' Yours for liberty.' "

"Another correspondent, who sends a subscription for $10,000, writes as follows :

" ' Need I say how delighted I am at the prospect of the ' PLAN OF FREEDOM?' In a work so just, so hopeful, so grandly comprehensive, so prophetic of results potential, victorious and final, I enter with a full soul, heart, hand and purse — and sink or swim, live or die, survive or perish, I give myself to this great work, in the full confidence that souls are here enlisted who know no tie but that of universal brotherhood — no ends but that of unselfish devotion to common humanity. May I ask of you the favor to hand in my subscription for one hundred shares of stock of the Massachusetts Emigrant Aid Company? The golden age — the blessed age of peace is not for us! Patience and faith and combat, labor and toil are ours. Let us accept the gifts meekly but manfully — rejoicing that our Master counts us worthy to follow him in the mighty travail of a world's regeneration.' "

From the New York *Tribune* of June 1, 1854 :

"THE PLAN OF FREEDOM.

" The friends of this measure who have had the subject in hand, held a meeting at the Astor House last evening, at which President King of

Columbia College presided. There was quite a full attendance of gentlemen who felt a deep interest in the subject. A committee was appointed to superintend the business of obtaining subscriptions, and to represent the subscribers in the meeting of the Society to be held in Boston on Wednesday next.

We are in receipt of additional letters, making inquiries and tendering further subscriptions. The plan is received by all with preëminent favor, and enlists the warmest sympathies of the friends of Freedom.

The plan is no less than to found free cities, and to extemporize free states. Let it be made the great enterprise of the age."

Other meetings were held in New York which were well attended, and subscriptions to a large amount were received. Among the largest subscribers were Horace B. Claflin and Rollin Sanford,— each six thousand dollars. In my efforts to stimulate as much as possible the interest, both commercial and philanthropic, which the cities of New York and Brooklyn had in making free states of Kansas and all our territories, I made on my first visit ten addresses — five in halls and five in private meetings of capitalists, like the one in Mr. Blunt's house. On two successive Friday evenings I addressed very enthusiastic audiences in Henry Ward Beecher's vestry. One Sunday Rev. Mr. Frothingham allowed me the use of his pulpit and the time allotted for his sermon, to make a speech for Kansas and free labor.

Later I had several conferences with William Cullen Bryant, and urged him to write editorials in his paper, the *Evening Post* — a financial organ of high authority — against the state bonds of Missouri every time the border ruffians raided Kansas. This he did on several occasions, and so well, that the bonds of the state, amounting to twenty millions, depreciated to such an extent that the holders interfered in every way they could to stop the raids, principally through the merchants of St. Louis. In consequence, the Missouri river was opened to our emigrants in the fall of 1856 after it had been closed all summer by the border ruffians.*

The above operations in New York extended over several months, but I have spoken of them here, as I may not have occasion to refer to them again. I will also say here that in the many different localities in which I spoke during the Kansas troubles, I never failed to interest the foremost influential men: Benjamin Silliman, of New Haven; Horace Bushnell, of Hartford; John Carter Brown, of Providence; the venerable Eliphalet Nott, at Albany; Joel Parker, Henry W. Longfellow, C. C. Felton, J. E. Worcester, Emory Washburn, John G. Palfrey and F. D. Huntington, of Cambridge; Josiah Quincy and William H. Prescott, of Boston, are representative names, and many others of equal weight can be adduced. The clergy were almost unanimous in their support and the scheme was greatly indebted to them for its success.

During my first visit to New York, news came from Boston, that the charter of the Massachusetts Emigrant Aid Company was thought to be defective; that some of the corporators feared that they might become personally responsible, and had withdrawn,† so that the undertaking was to be abandoned. This was a shock like a thunder-bolt, for I had anticipated nothing of the sort. Over one hundred thousand dollars had been subscribed in New York, and by the timidity of the Boston men all this was to be lost. I exerted myself in every possible way to prevent the surrender of the charter, but without avail, and I had to submit to the inevitable, with as good a grace as possible. I returned to Boston, where a voluntary organization was formed with a capital of two hundred thousand dollars under trustees, with Amos A. Lawrence, J. M. S. Williams and Eli Thayer as trustees. The new organization was known as the New England Emigrant Aid Company, and its operations were restricted in proportion as compared with those of the old company.

* See editorials in New York *Evening Post* of Feb. 14, 1856, and others about that time.
† This was a sad mistake, and it made the Rebellion possible.

Prof. Spring in his History of Kansas, says :   (page 30.)

" No organization was ever effected under the first charter.   It sad-
dled objectionable monetary liabilities upon the individuals who might
associate under it, and was abandoned.   The whole business then passed into the hands of Thayer, Lawrence and J. M. S. Williams,
who were constituted trustees, and managed affairs in a half personal fashion until February, 1855, when a second charter was obtained
and an association formed with a slightly rephrased title — ' The New
England Emigrant Aid Company ' — and with John Carter Brown, of
Providence, Rhode Island, as president.   In the conduct of the company, the trustees who bridged the interval between the first and
second charters, continued to be a chief directive and inspirational
force.   Mr. Thayer preached the gospel of organized emigration, with
tireless and successful enthusiasm, while Mr. Lawrence discharged the
burdensome but all important duties of treasurer.   Among the twenty
original directors were Dr. Samuel Cabot, Jr., John Lowell and
William B. Spooner, of Boston ; J. P. Williston, Northampton ;
Charles H. Bigelow, Lawrence ; and Nathan Durfee, Fall River.
The list of directors was subsequently enlarged to thirty-eight,
and included the additional names of Dr. S. G. Howe, Rev. Edward
Everett Hale, Boston ; George L. Stearns, Medford ; Horace Bushnell, Hartford, Connecticut ; Prof. Benjamin Silliman, Sr., New
Haven, Connecticut ; and Moses H. Grinnell, New York.   The company in its reorganized shape receded, at least, temporarily, from
all wholesale projects, and devoted itself to the problem of plant-
ing free-labor towns in Kansas." *

Although, greatly disappointed at the turn affairs had taken,
the managers were by no means discouraged, and they resolved
to persevere in the work.   Mr. Lawrence nobly pledged
himself to sustain the company by supplying the sinews

* The following is a full list of officers of the New England Emigrant Aid
Company :
PRESIDENT: John Carter Brown, *Providence;*   VICE-PRESIDENTS: Eli Thayer,
Worcester, J. M. S. Williams, *Cambridge;*   TREASURER: Amos A. Lawrence,
Boston; SECRETARY: Thomas H. Webb, *Boston;* DIRECTORS: Wm. B. Spooner,
Samuel Cabot, Jr., John Lowell, C. J. Higginson, Le Baron Russell, *Boston,*
Wm. J. Rotch, *New Bedford,* J. P. Williston, *Northampton,* W. Dudley Pick-
man, *Salem,* R. P. Waters, *Beverly,* Reuben A. Chapman, *Springfield,* John Nes-
mith, *Lowell,* Charles H. Bigelow, *Lawrence,* Nathan Durfee, *Fall River,* Wm.
Willis, *Portland, Me.,* Franklin Muzzy, *Bangor, Me.,* Ichabod Goodwin, *Ports-
mouth, N. H.,* Thomas M. Edwards, *Keene, N. H.,* Albert Day, *Hartford, Ct.*

of war to the extent of a very large sum, and others were not backward in this respect, though he was by far the largest contributor.*

When it was announced that Boston had decided to make a voluntary organization under trustees, with a possible capital of $200,000, the New York men said Boston could do that alone, and took no further part at that time. Mr. Greeley seemed also to lose heart, and said nothing more till the middle of June. In the New York *Tribune* of June 16, 1854, was printed the following :

"THE PLAN OF FREEDOM.

"All persons who desire particular information in relation to the plans, purposes and progress of the Emigrant Aid Company, are requested to send their communications to the 'Secretary of the Emigrant Aid Company,' Boston, Mass.

" We are informed that the Company intend to send the first train-load of emigrants to Kansas about the first of August next. The Company will forthwith forward mechanics and machinery for manufacturing lumber, and proceed to erect houses for emigrants.

" The Company is now organized, and books are opened for subscriptions to the capital stock. The original design of having so large a capital as five millions has been abandoned, and in lieu of annual contributions to the capital, as at first proposed, it is now designed to reduce the capital stock to the sum that will really be needed as an immediate working capital, and to change the character of the subscriptions, so that the whole amount of them shall be at the call of the trustees. It is now supposed that a paid-up capital of $200,000 will answer all the purposes of the Company. Such an alteration in the charter as this change necessitates, it is the intention of the Company to obtain immediately on the meeting of the Massachusetts Legislature. At the same time a change will be made in the title of the association, which will more fully denote the national character, and comport with the wide scope of its efforts."

I again entered upon the work with renewed courage, and spoke nightly, and sometimes oftener, to large and enthusiastic audiences. The effort now was to form a colony as soon as

---

* The Company expended about $140,000 in the Kansas work.

possible and start them on their way to carry freedom to Kansas. But few volunteered to join the first colony. After making a great number of speeches, after great efforts to influence by the strongest appeals the young men to join our colony, we had gathered a party numbering twenty-four; and on the 17th of July, 1854, I started with them towards Kansas. The colony was put on board a boat at Buffalo, having received an addition of two at Rochester.* To one of the emigrants — Mr. Mallory of Worcester — I gave a letter directed to Charles H. Branscomb (who with Charles Robinson had been sent on in advance to receive the emigrants at St. Louis) saying: " Take this colony through the Shawnee reservation and locate them on the south bank of the Kansas, on the first good town site you find west of the reservation." Mr. Branscomb followed literally the instructions of the letter and founded the city of Lawrence.

Leaving the colony at Buffalo, I returned to the East, and two weeks later the Company sent another colony several times larger than the first; and then the entire North and West began to be aroused, and to prepare to go if needed or to help others to go, and from this time the emigration continued to move on with increased activity. I was sent to raise colonies and to organize Kansas leagues, and I travelled all over New England, some parts of it more than once, and also spoke in all the principal places in New York State.

The effect of the influx of free state settlers into Kansas soon began to be manifested. What had at first been viewed by the Missourians with contempt and derision, and by many at the East with indifference, now became to the friends of the South a matter of serious alarm, and aroused the most malignant passions of the Missouri border ruffians. It created a feeling that spread through the entire slave-holding community, and excited an intense opposition towards a scheme which it was plain to them, was to establish an effectual barrier to the extension of slavery, and in time exterminate the institution. The South saw that it was impotent in a struggle of

* D. R. Anthony and Dr. Doy.

this kind with the North ; that the latter with its resources of wealth and population and its spirit of enterprise, would inevitably overwhelm them in this contest. All the powers of press and rostrum were brought to bear against the new scheme, and bluster and threats were resorted to in the endeavor to stem the current that was to engulf them. More extreme methods were applied on the scene of action, but it is not my purpose in this paper, to give any narration of what took place in Kansas ; that has already become a part of national history. Soon the greatest enthusiasm was excited in the North. Immense crowds gathered along the route of our emigrant companies, and the journeys through New England, and as far west as Chicago, were continued ovations. This spirit was shown even in the domestic circle. " I know people," said R. W. Emerson, " who are making haste to reduce their expenses and pay their debts, not with a view to new accumulations, but in preparation to save and earn for the benefit of Kansas emigrants."

The *Christian Examiner* of July, 1855, characterized the movement as follows :

"It was reserved to the present age and to the present period, to afford the sublime spectacle of an extensive migration in vindication of a principle. . . . . Neither pressure from without, nor the bickerings of ambition, nor the monitions of avarice control the great Kansas migration. . . . In the unselfishness of the object lies its claim . . to the highest place in the history of migrations!"

Loud threats of disunion were indulged in ; and the Southern papers teemed with abuse of the Emigrant Aid Company and its supporters. Rewards were offered for the head of the author of the plan.* But there were those among them,

* The following notice was posted in Kansas and Missouri:
"$200 Reward. We are authorized by responsible men in this neighborhood to offer the above reward for the apprehension and safe delivery into the hands of the squatters of Kansas Territory, of one Eli Thayer, a leading and ruling spirit among the abolitionists of New York and New England. Now, therefore, it behooves all good citizens of Kansas Territory and the State of Missouri, to watch the advent of this agent of Abolitionism — To arrest him, and deal with him in such a manner as

who, as the movement broadened, contemplated it in a more serious light, and gave evidence of their appreciation of the real character of the crisis. The following editorial from the Charleston *Mercury* well represents the views of this class :

" First. By consent of parties, the present contest in Kansas, is made the turning point in the destinies of slavery and abolitionism.* If the South triumphs, abolitionism will be defeated and shorn of its power for all time. If she is defeated, abolitionism will grow more insolent and aggressive, until the utter ruin of the South is consummated.

" Second. If the South secures Kansas, she will extend slavery into all the territory south of the fortieth parallel of north latitude, to the Rio Grande, and this, of course, will secure for her pent-up institutions of slavery an ample outlet, and restore her power in Congress. If the North secures Kansas, the power of the South in Congress will gradually be diminished, the states of Missouri, Kentucky, Tennessee, Arkansas and Texas, together with the adjacent territories, will gradually become abolitionized, and the slave population confined to the states east of the Mississippi will become valueless. All depends upon the action of the present moment. "

It may be well here to cite some further testimony as to the influence and work of the Emigrant Aid Company in establishing free colonies in Kansas.

In his evidence before the Howard Congressional Committee,† John H. Stringfellow, having been duly sworn, said :

" At the time of the passage of the Kansas-Nebraska Bill and prior to that time, I never heard any man, in my section of Missouri, express a doubt about the character of the institutions which would be established here, provided the Missouri restriction was removed ; and I heard of no combination of persons, either in public or private, prior to the time of the organization of the Emigrant Aid Society, and indeed

the enormity of his crimes and iniquities shall seem to merit. Representing *all* the Abolitionists, he consequently bears all their sins; and the blood of Batchelder is upon his head crying aloud for expiation at the hands of the people."

DeBow's Review called the movement "Thayer's Emigration ; " and the Southern press spoke of the Emigrant Aid Company as " Eli Thayer & Co." — ED.

* By "abolitionism" the editor intended the whole anti-slavery element. He had no reference to Garrisonism

† House Doc., 34th Congress, No. 200.

for months afterwards, for the purpose of making united action, to frustrate the designs of that Society in abolitionizing, or making a free state of Kansas. The conviction was general, that it would be a slave state. The settlers who came over from Missouri after the passage of the Bill, so far as I know, generally believed that Kansas would be a slave state. Free-state men who came into the territory after the passage of the bill were regarded with jealousy by the people of western Missouri, for the reason that a society had been formed for the avowed purpose of shaping the institutions of Kansas Territory, so as to make it a free state in opposition to the interests of the people of Missouri. If no Emigrant Aid Societies had been formed in the Northern States, the emigration of people from there, known to be in favor of making Kansas a free state, would have stimulated the emigration from Missouri. Had it not been for the Emigrant Aid Societies, the majority in favor of slave institutions would, by the natural course of emigration, have been so great as to have fixed the institutions of the Territory without any exciting contest, as it was in the Settlement of the Platte Purchase. This was the way we regarded the passage of the Kansas-Nebraska Bill, and this was the reason why we supported it."

Isaac M. Edwards: (sworn.)

" It is my opinion that all the difficulties and troubles have been produced by the operations of the Emigrant Aid Society. I am satisfied that if the Emigrant Aid Society had not sent men out to the Territory of Kansas for the purpose of making it a free state, there would be no trouble or difficulties in the Territory. "

Scores of other witnesses before the Howard Commission testified in nearly the same words, that there would have been *no contest whatever in Kansas*, had it not been caused by the efforts of the Emigrant Aid Company to make Kansas a free state, by sending thither organized colonies of free-state men.

This was not the testimony of Missourians alone, nor of proslavery settlers in Kansas. You will find it in all the proslavery papers of the time and in nearly all the anti-slavery journals.

Throughout the South, the Emigrant Aid Company, often under the name of " Eli Thayer & Co.," was charged with the enormous crime of making Kansas a free state. In Missouri, various sums, in several localities, were publicly offered for the head of the founder of that Company.

Even in the Halls of Congress, pro-slavery senators and representatives denounced this Company as the power which had robbed the slave-state party of Kansas, and had put in peril the very existence of slavery.

In 1861, though the battle had been fought in Kansas and the victory won by the free-state men years before, Senator Green, of Missouri, said in the Senate : " But for the hot-bed plants that have been planted in Kansas, through the instrumentality of the Emigrant Aid Society, Kansas would have been with Missouri this day. "

Stephen A. Douglas, in his report to the U. S. Senate, in 1856, said : "Popular Sovereignty was struck down by unholy combinations in New England. "

Senator J. A. Bayard, of Delaware, said : " Whatever evil, or loss, or suffering, or injury, may result to Kansas, or to the United States at large, is attributable, as a primary cause, to the Emigrant Aid Society of Massachusetts. "

If further testimony be needed to show the power of the Emigrant Aid Company in Kansas, it can be found in quantities almost without limit, in the Congressional Globe, in the reports of Congressional Committees, in thousands upon thousands of letters from the Kansas settlers to their friends in the states, in the editorials of all the Southern and of nearly all the Northern journals, in the reports of thousands of election speeches, and in all contemporaneous and general records of whatever kind.

While the Emigrant Aid Company, was, by its operations, creating such a well-founded alarm in the Southern States, and was receiving the commendation and gratitude of every true lover of freedom for the practical results it had accomplished, let us see how it was regarded by that peculiar clique, known as the Garrisonian Abolitionists. At the time of the repeal of the Missouri Compromise, and the passage of the Kansas-Nebraska Bill, these men had been absolutely silent ; and in the period of

gloom and despair at the North that followed that iniquity, they
had no words, either of counsel, encouragement or commisera-
·tion, to offer. No sooner, however, was a feasible and practical plan of retrieving the disaster set forth, than Mr. Garrison
and his associates opened their batteries of vituperation upon it
and its authors, as they had always assailed every practical and
feasible measure, and everybody who proposed to DO something
for the cause of freedom ; and as they continued to assail everybody and every thing except DISUNION, until in *spite* of them
and without their aid, the great object was achieved, when they
and their admirers turned about and coolly said : We did all
this ourselves ! The present generation has, in consequence of
the persistent clack and endless scribbling of that class, come to
believe that Mr Garrison was the Alpha and Omega of the anti-
slavery struggle, and that he and his small party of followers
were the leaders and directors of the great movement that
brought about the overthrow of Slavery. These men and
women have never exhibited any diffidence or modesty in
sounding their own praises. They formed a mutual admiration
society of unusual malignity towards those who did not belong
to it ; yet, not content with fighting the outside world, they fre-
quently snarled and quarrelled among themselves, and attempted to destroy each other. The persecution they endured was
not wholly on account of the Anti-Slavery principles they
maintained, but it was their abusive and insulting manner, and
particularly, their offensive obtrusion of the unpopular and un-
patriotic doctrines of secession and disunion upon every occasion, that principally excited the passions of the mob.

In fact, the little company of Abolitionists had come to be
despised at the North, and they were neglected and shunned by
the better element for the reasons above given. Almost invariably in presenting my plan of emigration, the question would
come, Has Garrison anything to do with this? Is there any
taint of abolitionism in it? and I had to assure my hearers
that it was entirely free from that objectionable element. However, as Mr. Garrison and his friends have been elevated into
such a prominent position, and as an exaggerated and distorted

idea of their services largely prevails, some even believing that
they aided in the saving of Kansas, it is proper for me to show
here, in what manner they viewed an undertaking which had for
its object the extermination of Slavery by peaceful, lawful and
practical methods, and how they treated those who honestly and
earnestly gave to it their support. The following extracts and
quotations, will show their kind of wisdom and power of
prophecy.

Mr. Garrison (*Liberator*, 30th June, 1854, commenting on
the address to the people by the anti-Nebraska members of
Congress), says :

" If this is all that is proposed to be done, the address will prove
utterly abortive. To talk of ' restoring the Missouri Compromise' and
preventing ' the further aggressions of Slavery ' while the Union holds
together, is the acme of infatuation. *We must separate.* The North
must form a new, independent, free republic, or continue to be the tool
and vassal of the Slave Power, making it to accomplish all its direful
designs of conquest, annexation and perpetuation, having the mighty
resources of the whole country at its command, without which it
would be as poor as a pauper and as feeble as an infant." *

In the *Liberator* of Feb. 16, 1855, is a letter from its correspondent, C. Stearns, dated, Lawrence, Kansas, Jan. 20, 1855,
in which we find this :

" It is true we denounce the Emigrant Aid Company, because we
believe it to be a great hindrance to the cause of freedom, and a mighty
curse to the Territory ; but we are the only ones who have taken a
decided ground on the anti-slavery question. I have never heard of
the Lawrence Association ever passing any anti-slavery resolutions.

" Another point of importance is, that this association, with Robinson at its head, advocates brute force in opposing the Missourians.
Said Mr. R. to the Marshal, in reference to some Missourians arrested
for threatening the Yankees, ' If they fire, do you make them bite the
dust and I will find coffins.' "

In a letter one month later, published in the *Liberator* of the
16th of March, 1855, the same correspondent says :

* Compare this with the resolution in which they say that slavery can grow and
fatten upon the territory already secured to it for ages to come.

"Do not advise people to emigrate here in companies. Let them come very few at a time. This sending large companies is a very foolish business for many reasons."

In another paper Mr. Garrison says, in substance : Kansas cannot be made a free state, and even if it should be, such a result would be a great injury to the anti-slavery cause, for the reason that it would quiet the Northern conscience. The following is from the *Liberator* (editorial) of June 1, 1855 :

"Will Kansas be a free state? We answer—No. Not while the existing Union stands. Its fate is settled. We shall briefly state some of the reasons which force us to this sad conclusion.

"1. The South is united in the determination to make Kansas a slave state—ultimately, by division, half a dozen slave states, if necessary. She has never yet been foiled in her purposes thus concentrated and expressed, and she has too much at stake to allow free speech, a free press, and free labor, to hold the mastery in that Territory.

"2. Eastern emigration will avail nothing to keep slavery out of Kansas. We have never had any faith in it as a breakwater against the inundation of the dark waters of oppression. Hardly an abolitionist can be found among all who have emigrated to that country.* Undoubtedly the mass of emigrants are in favor of making Kansas a free state, as a matter of sound policy, and would do so if they were not under the dominion of Missouri ruffianism, or if they could rely upon the sympathy of the general government in this terrible crisis, but they have not gone to Kansas to be martyrs in the cause of the enslaved negro, nor to sacrifice their chances for a homestead upon the altar of principle, but to find a comfortable home for themselves and their children. Before they emigrated they gave little or no countenance to the anti-slavery cause at home † : they partook of the general hostility or indifference to the labors of radical abolitionism ; at least they could only dream of making ' freedom national and slavery sectional after the manner of the fathers ; ' ‡ and they were poisoned more or less with the virus of colorphobia. If they had no pluck here, what could be rationally expected of them in the immediate presence of the demoniacal spirit of slavery? They represent the average sentiment of the North §

* This was literally true ; there was not a Garrisonian among them.
† That is, to Mr. Garrison's peculiar dogmas.
‡ A fling at Charles Sumner.
§ A thoughtless and careless admission by Mr. Garrison that his labors had amounted to nothing.

on this subject — nothing more — and that is still subservient to the will of the South.

.

" 3. The omnipotent power of the general government will coöperate with the vandals of Missouri to crush out what little anti-slavery sentiment may exist in Kansas, and to sustain their lawless proceedings in that Territory. This will prove decisive in the struggle.*

" 4. On the subject of slavery there is no principle in the Kansas papers ostensibly desirous of making it a free state. Here, for instance, is the *Herald of Freedom* of May 12th, published in Lawrence, which claims to be, and we believe is, the most outspoken journal in Kansas in regard to the rights of *bona-fide* settlers. What does its editor say? Listen! ' While publishing a paper in Kansas, we feel that it is not our province to discuss the subject of freedom or slavery in the States.' † Is not this the most heartless inhumanity, the most arrant, moral cowardice, the clearest demonstration of unsoundness of mind?

" These are some of the reasons why we believe Kansas will inevitably be a slave state."

Liberator, Sept. 28, 1855. Editorial :

" Talk about stopping the progress of slavery and of saving Nebraska and Kansas! Why the fate of Nebraska and Kansas was sealed the first hour Stephen Arnold Douglas consented to play his perfidious part."

In the *Liberator* of August 10, 1855, is a speech of Wendell Phillips, from which the following is extracted :

* Did it prove so ?
† G. W. Brown established the *Herald of Freedom*, and maintained it as the organ of the Emigrant Aid Company through the Kansas troubles. It was ever true to the principle and purpose of making Kansas a Free State. Mr. Garrison and his friends complained because the editor refused to enter into controversy upon the general subject of Slavery in the States, and would not fill his columns with "Resolutions" and complaints about blood-hounds, manacles and auction blocks. The paper was ably conducted, and was of inestimable value to the cause in furnishing and disseminating information about the Territory, much of which was given by the actual settlers. The Emigrant Aid Company advanced $3000 to aid Dr. Brown in establishing this journal, which sum he repaid. Dr. Brown knew "Old John Brown" intimately while he was in Kansas, and his reminiscences of that worthy, published a few years since, created something of a stampede among the admirers of the Hero of Harper's Ferry.

" Why Is Kansas a failure as a free state? I will tell you. You sent out there some thousand or two thousand men — for what ? To make a living; to cultivate a hundred and sixty acres; to build houses; to send for their wives and children; to raise wheat; to make money; to build saw mills; to plant towns. You meant to take possession of the country, as the Yankee race always takes possession of a country, by industry, by civilization, by roads, by houses, by mills, by churches; but it will take a long time — *it takes two centuries to do it.**

.   .   .   .

" The moment you throw the struggle with slavery into the half-barbarous West, where things are decided by the revolver and bowie knife, slavery triumphs.

" What do I care for a squabble around the ballot-box in Kansas ?" [!!!]

Liberator, 2d May, 1856. Meeting of A. A. Society at Providence, R. I. Mr. Garrison said :

" While the Union continues, the slave power will have everything its own way, in the last resort.

" ' But (they say) we are going to have a glorious victory in Kansas.'

" It is all delusion to suppose that Kansas is safe for freedom. † We are just to late ! † We have been betrayed by the general government itself, which is now on the side of ' border ruffianism !' Slavery is certain to go into Kansas, nay, slaves are now carried there daily. and offered for sale with impunity. Even the free state men have voted to let slavery continue in the Territory till the 4th of July next, and that no colored man shall be allowed to set his foot upon the soil of Kansas; thus trampling under foot the Constitution of the United States. " ‡

Annual statement adopted at the May Convention of the A. A. S., Massachusetts, 1856 :

" Yet we cannot conceal it from ourselves that the too probable result will be, if Kansas be secured to freedom, that the vile American spirit of *compromise* will take possession of its counsels, control its

* This was a remarkable prophecy.
† Before this, in speaking of the movements in Kansas it had been " *You* " with Mr. Garrison. When, however, it became evident that Kansas was sure to be secured to freedom, he speedily changed his " you " to " *We*. "
‡ Patriotic Mr. Garrison! How he loved the Constitution of his country!

internal affairs, and govern its intercourse with the neighboring slave states; while, as a still more lamentable consequence, apathy will settle upon the whole Northern mind, satisfied with their seeming victory, but the end of which will be only to invite fresh insults and aggressions from the Southern despotism. No! there is no safety as there is no honor and no right in our union with men-stealers. No advantage gained while in that fatal fellowship can be of any value."

From a speech of Wendell Phillips, printed in the *Liberator* of July 11, 1856 :

"Now I have great hopes.* I think Fremont will be defeated. I think there is great chance that Buchanan will be elected. I have no hope for Kansas. How can I have? Where are the hundred men who went from Chicago? Why, they went through Missouri, and laid down their arms at the feet of a mob! Fifty men from the city of Worcester met the same fate. A thousand dollars from the town of Concord alone, gone into the treasury of the Missouri mob! . . . . Fifty per cent. of the muskets bought in New England are to-day in the hands of Missourians."†

From a speech of Wendell Phillips, printed in the *Liberator* of August 14, 1857 :

"But Kansas — her battle will not be fought in the West, but on the chess-board at Washington, and in midnight session she will be betrayed. This administration will see Kansas, possibly Oregon and Nebraska, possibly the southern half of California — admitted as slave states; and then, with four or six more votes in the Senate, with the prestige of success, how will you meet another Presidential election?"‡

Rev. T. W. Higginson, minister of the Worcester Free Church, said : (See *Liberator* of June 16, 1854)

"Here, for instance, is the Nebraska Emigration Society; it is indeed a noble enterprise, and I am proud that it owes its origin to a Worcester man. But where is the good of emigrating to Nebraska, if Nebraska is to be only a transplanted Massachusetts, and the original Massachusetts has been tried and found wanting?"

* Most rational men would not have had "great hopes" in the face of the crisis he portrayed.
† This well exhibits the ridiculous style of exaggeration which characterized the utterances of the Abolitionists.
‡ Here was another remarkable prophecy.

Liberator, 16th May, 1856, 23d anniversay of the A. A. Society, New York city. Mr. Garrison offered this among other resolutions which was unanimously passed :

" *Resolved* : That (making all due allowance for exceptional cases) the American Church continues to be the bulwark of Slavery, and threfore impure in heart, hypocritical in profession, dishonest in practice, brutal in spirit, merciless in purpose,—' a cage of unclean birds' and ' the synagogue of Satan.' "

At the same meeting Samuel May, Jr., said :

"That he thought that both duty, and a sound and just expediency utterly forbade our identifying ourselves, for an instant, with the mere *non*-extension-of-Slavery-movement. Especially would he protest against our identifying ourselves, as a Society, with the Kansas free state movement, so long as it stands upon its present low and compromising level. . . . .
"We cannot join in the present movement for Kansas because *it is false in principle*. That is a sufficient reasou why we should take uo part in it."

Here is another of Mr. Garrison's resolutions against the church :

"*Resolved* : That such a church is, in the graphic language of Scripture ' a cage of unclean birds' and the 'synagogue of satan,' and that such religious teachers are 'wolves in sheep's clothing,' ' Watchmen that are blind,' ' Shepherds that cannot understand,' ' that all look to their own way, every one to his gain from his quarter.' "

This is a good specimen of Mr. Garrison's utterances against those who would not endorse and countenance his own unreasonable and sensational doctrines. Among those whom he characterizes as " unclean birds," may be mentioned Leonard Bacon, Eliphalet Nott, Horace Bushnell, Henry Ward Beecher, Edward Everett Hale, and the 3,050 clergymen of the North who protested against the passage of the Kansas-Nebraska bill. It was this kind of abuse that more than anything else brought the Abolitionists into disrepute. After reading the above

extracts it is not necessary to say that they not only did nothing
to save Kansas, but opposed all the efforts of others to make it
a free state.

Unfortunately the Garrisonians were not the only ones who
whined and carped at the condition of affairs. Many at the
North were involved in the gloom of despondency and were dis-
posed to look upon the contest between Freedom and Slavery
with doubt as to the result. The managers of the Emigrant
Aid enterprise did not participate in this feeling, but prosecuted
their work with a firm conviction that Slavery would be overcome. In 1856, when doleful predictions were made, that if
Buchanan was elected, Kansas would be lost, I said in a public
speech in Worcester: " It will make no difference whether Fremont, Buchanan or the devil is President. Kansas is going to
be a Free State anyhow." At a dinner at Mr. Seward's in
Washington, some time before, I rather startled the guests, who
were mostly Republicans, by proclaiming that under any circumstances there would never be another slave state in this
Union—NEVER! In my speeches in Congress and elsewhere,
between 1856 and 1861, I always treated Slavery as a " mori-
bund institution." I do not speak of this with any idea of self-
glorification, but I mention it because it was a fact. From the
time that the first colony was successfully planted in Kansas, I
felt sure of the cause, and when the first tidings of lawless aggression against the settlers came, I KNEW that the death knell
of Slavery was sounded. The old Saxon spirit, so long dor-
mant and forbearing under insult and persecution when committed within the law, could not brook this wilful outrage, and it
needed but this spark to arouse its fury.

The Latin races claim that their founders were nursed by a
wolf. The Saxons have a higher origin. Their founder was
nursed by a polar bear. Deep in the nature of this race is
found that untamable ferocity, which fears nothing, but can
endure everything.

It was no Saxon sculptor who chiseled Prometheus writhing in
torture, while the vulture fed upon his vitals. A Latin but not a
Saxon could make a Laocoön showing pitiable contortions of

feature and of limb, in the embrace of the serpents. A Saxon in both cases, would have shown a calm and defiant endurance, affording neither comfort nor exultation to the tormentor.

This sublime endurance, this proud defiance, this unvarying courage, all based on a sort of savage ferocity, give assurance that the Saxons will make law and language for the world. These qualities may be usually concealed under the various coverings of all the Christian amenities. We may appear to be perfect examples of amiable submission, and of Christian humility. We may be sympathetic or even philanthropic; but under all this gentle and genial exterior, there slumbers the grizzly ferocity. It is in every Saxon breast. The old blind poet of England knew all this, when he made the hero of Paradise Lost—

" With courage never to submit or yield,
And what is more not to be overcome."

A hundred baptisms cannot drown it; a thousand sacraments cannot eliminate it. It was with Cromwell and his Ironsides. Wellington felt it as he stood under the elm at Waterloo and received unmoved the repeated charges of Ney and the Imperial Guard. In peace and in war, this quality is found wherever there is Saxon blood. Hampden and Sydney and Gordon and millions of others have illustrated it. It fills histories. It makes libraries. It remodels nations. It will govern the world.

In 1856 this ferocious quality was fully aroused in the Northern States. We had long endured, with calmness and patience, the aggressions of the Slave Power when made according to law. But these later aggressions against all law, we would not endure. The North became a unit against slavery in Kansas. The North triumphed and Slavery was destroyed.

One other matter and I will close.

In 1879 the Twenty-fifth Anniversary of the founding of Lawrence, Kansas, was celebrated by a reunion of the early settlers and others connected with the first Kansas movement. The occasion was one of great interest, and naturally many recollections and reminiscences were exchanged, some of which found their way into newspapers. The press of the country reviewed the great struggle which saved Kansas for freedom, and awarded due credit to the Emigrant Aid Company as the prime force in that movement. This brought out the following from a "Radical Abolitionist," which appeared in the Boston *Daily Advertiser* of September 9th, 1879 :

"*To the Editor of the Boston Daily Advertiser:*

" Will you allow one who was not unfamiliar with the early Kansas emigration to criticise your two valuable editorials on that subject as being written too exclusively from the point of view of the 'Emigrant Aid Society.'

" No one can deny the important influence exerted by that association, though it always seemed to me that its 'organized emigration' in a strict sense, was a failure, as must be all attempts to control from a distance the settlement of a new community. Its associated emigrants were apt to separate on reaching Kansas.

" When its saw-mills broke down there had to be negotiations across half the continent before they could be repaired; and meanwhile private enterprise had perhaps set up a better saw-mill not far off.

" What the 'Society' really did was to advertise Kansas, and to direct thither a really superior class of settlers. This was a very important first step. But these early settlers were, like most Northern men at that period, men of peace. When civil war came, new leaders had to come to the front, and new instrumentalities proved necessary. The real crisis of Kansas was in 1856, after your brief record terminates. That year brought a state of things in which the 'Emigrant Aid Society' was practically paralyzed, and it was necessary to form new organizations which had no objection to buying Sharp's rifles. The formation of these 'Kansas Committees' in the free states, and the leadership of Brown, Lane and Montgomery within the territory, were what finally saved Kansas to freedom.

" But for these influences the Missourian invasion would have swept away every trace of the 'Emigrant Aid Society' and its work.

" My criticism of your series of articles is, therefore, that they stop where the real Kansas trouble began.

" CAMBRIDGE.   " T. W. H "

The author of the above is said to be a writer of "Pure English," but there is one thing about this production purer than its English, and that is, its nonsense. The qualities of a

"professional novelist" are not quite submerged in the amateur
historian, and the above induces the belief that its author would
make Charles Lee the hero of the battle of Monmouth. Should
he ever enlarge the sphere of his labors so as to include the
writing of sacred history, we shall probably learn that Barabbas
and the two thieves were the founders of the Christian religion.
As for Brown, Lane and Montgomery, we will leave them
where Professor Spring, in his History of Kansas, leaves them ;
and posterity will find them there in all future time.

In regard to the "New Organizations," and "Kansas Committees," it probably did not occur to "T. W. H." that there
would have been no occasion for such bodies had it not been for
the foundation laid by the Emigrant Aid Company. They sustained the same relation to that body as the branches of a tree
do to its trunk and roots. If it was his purpose to rob those
connected with the Emigrant Aid Company of their just credit
by giving the impression that they were not concerned in the
later organizations which he claims saved Kansas, the following
from the Boston *Daily Advertiser* of July 17, 1856, will show
how trustworthy are his premises :

[Leading Editorial.]
"THE SYSTEMATIC RELIEF OF KANSAS.

"The arrangements made last week at the national convention at
Buffalo, of the friends of Kansas, for giving system to the general
desire of the northern states to assist the free men of Kansas, are such
as promise an immediate concentration of action and seem to us to
evince great practical wisdom.

"For this purpose the convention named the national executive
committee, having a quorum of its members in the city of Chicago, to
act as a disbursing committee of the funds collected in the different
parts of the country for the benefit of Kansas settlers and emigrants.

⋅ ⋅ ⋅ ⋅ ⋅ ⋅ ⋅ ⋅

"For the object, equally important, of securing a universal contri-
bution to these funds, the convention adopted a measure which also
has our decided approval. On motion of Mr. Gerrit Smith, Mr. Eli
Thayer of this state, was appointed a committee of one to take charge
of the systematic organization of all the states friendly to Kansas, for
her relief. We believe the convention was wise in making this com-

mittee consist of one person. We believe it particularly fortunate in appointing Mr. Thayer to a duty which he can discharge so efficiently. The service which he has rendered to Kansas, first by creating the Emigrant Aid Company, in the face of great depression, and next, by constant public and private appeals in behalf of Kansas, is well understood in New England and New York city. The work now entrusted to him is very clearly the work for one man and not for many.

"We are glad to be able to announce this morning, that Mr. Thayer has already entered upon his work, with the promptness which the occasion demands.

"He has perfected a plan which may carry the cause of Kansas to every hearth-stone in the free states.

"It proposes that there shall be formed two classes of Kansas Committees; a state committee for every state, and a county committee for every county. Some of these committees already exist. Each county committee should then appoint a town agent for every town in the county, with authority to appoint a solicitor (male or female) for every school district in the town. These district solicitors apply to every man, woman and child, if possible, in their respective districts; and make returns of their collections, with a duplicate of the subscription books, to the town agent. By applying to this agent, any subscriber can ascertain whether his subscription has been duly forwarded. The town agents make returns to the treasurer of the County Committee, who makes regular returns to the treasurer of the State Committee, who in turn remits to the National Committee.

"In this way every cent contributed can be traced from the hand of the donor to the treasury of the General Committee, without any charge or expenses. And by this plan the General Committee deals only with State Committees, these with County Committees, and these only with school districts, and they only with individuals.

"If this plan were faithfully carried out, we should have three or four millions of subscribers as the result, with scarcely any expense for agencies.

"We publish these details, in extenso, thus, in the hope that they may be at once copied through the country, and that the different arrangements may be put at once in motion. We hope to announce soon, that a regular series of remittances to the Chicago National Committee has begun.

"We observed in our report of the Buffalo Convention, that a member of that convention expressed the feeling that Mr. Thayer's connection with the Emigrant Aid Company would make his appointment unpopular with the country. We confess our surprise at this suggestion. We believe that the unanimous feeling of the free states of this Union

towards that company, of which he is the founder, is one of profound
gratitude for its efforts at a time when every one beside was in despair
as to the fate of Kansas.

"The Convention at Buffalo would never have existed, had not that
company acted when it did.   There would have been no free state
party in Kansas without it.   There may be many men there from the
free states who did not go under its auspices, but there are very few
who did not go influenced by the assurance that the company gave,
that Kansas should be free.

"We can understand why President Pierce and Dr. Stringfellow denounce it; but we do not see why the unpopularity of its founder *with
them* should act in the Buffalo Convention.

"Mr. Thayer defended the company with spirit before the Convention, and the Convention showed no fear of its unpopularity.   He
referred to the enthusiastic praise it has received abroad and at home.
Styled by the London *Times* 'The greatest American movement of
this age,' it has been welcomed here by our ablest statesmen, scholars
and business men.

"After his speech no sort of opposition was made to his appointment; and the Convention commissioned him to the work we have
described."

This Buffalo Convention was composed of delegates from the
Kansas Leagues throughout the North and East.   These
Leagues were formed entirely through the influence of the
Emigrant Aid Company.   About five hundred representatives
attended the convention.   The delegates from Worcester were
Dwight Foster, George F. Hoar and Eli Thayer.

As for "Sharpe's rifles," I know many went along with the
emigrants sent by the Company, and these men knew how
to use them when the emergency demanded, as those familiar
with Kansas history well know.   No organization *openly* provided such implements at first, but they generally formed a part
of the equipment of our colonies.   The directors furnished them
on their individual responsibility.   Mr. Lawrence and others of
the Company provided a large quantity of arms and ammunition
and sent them to Kansas in 1855.*   I, myself, bought two
cases of rifles of Waters & Co., in the spring of 1855, months

* See Transactions Kansas Historical Society, Vols. I. and II., pp. 221-224.

before " T. W. II.'s " " Later organizations " were thought of. *
These went to Kansas.

The complaint of the Abolitionists themselves, early in 1855,
that we were ready to repel force by force, is a sufficient refuta-
tion of the insinuation that the early emigrants would not fight.
But they did not believe in shedding blood wantonly. Dr. Robinson's firm and decided policy, and the fact that the settlers
were well armed with *Sharpe's rifles* and ready to use them,
caused the retreat of the Missourians from Lawrence in December, 1855. Probably " T. W. II. " did not know of these facts.

Again, I would ask " T. W. H." if it is reasonable for him to
maintain, that private enterprise would be better provided with
tools and materials to repair broken-down saw-mills, than a
well-organized corporation with managers who took into consideration all the wants, needs and circumstances of the undertaking?

Professor Spring in his History of Kansas, says : (page 32)

" The work of the Boston organizat'on cannot be adequately exhibited by arithmetical computations. A vital, capital part of it lay
in spheres where mathematics are ineffectual—lay in its alighting upon
a feasible method, which was copied far and wide, of dealing with
a grave political emergency, and in the backing of social and monetary
prestige that it secured for the unknown pioneers at the front. "

The work of saving Kansas, was done before the eyes of the
whole world. We said we would do it, and stop the making of
Slave States. We also laid down our methods ; we went on
just as we had promised and used the methods proposed, and
accomplished the results aimed at, without the help of politicians,
and in spite of the active hostility of the abolitionists.

No man, unless he is ignorant of the facts in the Kansas
struggle, or is completely blinded by malice or envy, will ever
attempt to defraud the Emigrant Aid Company of the glory of
having saved Kansas, by defeating the Slave Power, in a great
and decisive contest.

* During the Kansas troubles I expended of my own money $4,500 for the pur-
chase of rifles and cannon.

The results of the Kansas contest may be briefly summarized :

1. It stopped the making of Slave States.
2. It made the Republican Party.
3. It nearly elected Fremont and *did* elect Lincoln.
4. It united and solidified the Northern states against slavery, and was a necessary training, to enable them to subdue the Rebellion. *
5. It drove the slave-holders, through desperation, into secession.
6. It has given us a harmonious and enduring Union.
7. It has emancipated the white race of the South, as well as the negroes, from the evils of Slavery.
8. It is even now regenerating the South.

In 1854, there floated, in careless security, the staunch old battle-ship SLAVERY. She was then undisputed mistress of all American waters For more than thirty years, she had been victorious in every contest. She had seen the power of her enemies constantly diminishing, while her own had been constantly increasing. At this time, from the top of her tallest mast, was displayed the broad pennant of the Commodore — from the other masts floated other pennants and streamers bearing the legends of her many victories. On one was the inscription

* The wonderful increase of the Anti-Slavery vote in '55 and '56 was brought about by the illegal assaults of the Slave power upon the citizens of Kansas. The figures in New England and New York from 1848 to 1856 are here given. It will be seen that the fall elections of 1854 were little influenced by the repeal of the Missouri Compromise.

	NEW ENGLAND	NEW YORK.
1848	72,368	120,479
1849	79,454	1,311
1850	42,270	3,410
1851	43,401	000
1852	57,143	25,359
1853	63,668	000
(Repeal of the Missouri Compromise, a *Lawful* act.)		
1854	79,632	000
(After *Unlawful* aggression in Kansas.)		
1855	184,850	136,698
1856	307,417	276,004

" The Admission of Texas ; " on another, " The Fugitive
Slave Bill : " there " The Dred Scott Decision ; " while here
was haughtily displayed, the record of her latest triumph " The
Repeal of the Missouri Compromise." Her officers, in com.
placent mood, were proudly pacing her decks, recounting the
unvarying success of the past, and laying plans for new triumphs in the future : — Cuba to be acquired ; Central America
and Mexico to be secured ; and all to be devoted to the building
up of a colossal slave empire.

While in this blissful security, in this paradise of memory
and hope, a billow from Boston harbor struck her side. It was
not a heavy wave, but it made the old ship tremble and aroused
the attention of officers and crew. All hands on board soon
had enough to do. Billow after billow came.

For three whole years these bounding billows came with
increasing strength and most destructive force, while the brave
old ship pitched and groaned and quivered more and more with
each successive shock. Her joints were loosened and the waters
rushed in. Her officers were utterly disheartened and ran her
for safety upon the shoals of Secession. At length the dark
waves of the Rebellion swept her fragments away, and not one
vestige was left in 1865, of the famous craft, which was queen
of all American waters in 1854.

That staunch old battle-ship was the hideous " Black Power "
which had ruled the United States with despotic sway, for more
than thirty years. The billows which struck her, were the self-
sacrificing organized colonies of sturdy Northern Yeomen, who
had determined that Slavery should be no more. These were
the billows that destroyed the old ship.

But some say it was not the billows at all, but the foam on
their crests that made the wreck. Some say it was not the
thousands upon thousands of brave patriotic Union-loving citizens, organized for this very work, and risking their all for
Freedom, that brought this speedy end to Slavery, but that it
was three or four adventurers and sensationalists — all haters of
the Union and friends of anarchy — that achieved this great
victory. Let the country judge upon the evidence of the facts.